HACCP in training
Food safety principles made easy

Dagmar Engel

Chadwick
House
Group
Limited

ISBN 1-902423-54-2

Chadwick House Group Limited
Chadwick Court
15 Hatfields
London
SE1 8DG
England

Publications Tel: 020 7827 5882
Fax: 020 7827 9930
Email: Publications@chgl.com
www.cieh.org

Chadwick House Group Ltd is the trading subsidiary of the Chartered Institute of Environmental Health (CIEH), the professional and educational body for those who work in environmental health in England, Wales and Northern Ireland. Founded in 1883, the Chartered Institute has charitable status and its primary function is the promotion of knowledge and understanding of environmental health issues.

Contents

Appendices

PREFACE

Learning is finding out what you already know.

Doing is demonstrating that you know it.

Teaching is reminding others that they know just as well as you.

You are all learners, doers, teachers.

You teach best what you most need to learn.

(R. Bach)

'HACCP is all about doing. In fact HACCP is much easier to do than read or write about' (Mitchell, 1995). Why then have I written a book on HACCP training?

Since the early days of the HACCP concept when NASA and Pillsbury came together to work out a safety system to protect astronauts from food poisoning and food-borne infections, hundreds of publications have been issued trying to describe HACCP. From highly academic explications to technical manuals, many authors have tried to put the original idea into words. The longer the HACCP system exists and the more its implementation is not only recommended but also required, the more complicated it seems to become – very much to the annoyance of small and medium-sized businesses who are nowadays confronted with the need to implement the principles of a system that seems far too 'scientific' for the average food-handler.

The easiest way to make a simple concept complicated is to use technological terms and scientific semantics. Like every new concept, HACCP introduces a number of definitions such as 'hazard', 'risk', 'severity', 'verification', etc. It should always be the ambition of a good HACCP consultant or HACCP team trainer to make these definitions transparent and easy to understand. There are certainly ways around this, but it needs common sense *and* a good trainer to free HACCP from the ivory tower of science.

Since the recommendations laid down in *Training Aspects of the Hazard Analysis Critical Control Point System* by the World Health Organisation (WHO) in 1996 the standard of HACCP training courses has gained more and more importance. As HACCP is a matter that concerns every staff member, it is the aspects of understanding and communicating in particular which determine the system's acceptance and efficiency on the shop floor. To provide a thorough understanding it is essential to keep the slogan 'HACCP is all about *doing*' in your mind. This means that HACCP training courses need to be as practical as possible.

Bearing in mind that we have to deal with adult learners, HACCP training needs to fit the adult learning scheme. Adult learners are much more self-directing than the more dependent child learner – they want to see an almost immediate benefit following the chores of the learning experience. HACCP theory needs to be interpreted and adjusted to the individual situation on the shop floor. Its practical and, hopefully, successful application will strengthen confidence in the system and success means positive experience which is both confirming and encouraging.

This is not the first or only HACCP training guide. Why then should you read it? What is it that makes this book different?

In short, this book

- stresses the interactive quality of HACCP training;

- focuses on communicative aspects between trainer and trainees;

- offers and describes different training methods and motivation techniques;

- gives provocative ideas to keep your trainees alert and interested.

After an introductory chapter which discusses the importance of understanding HACCP and illustrates some of the pitfalls in teaching it, the book is set out in two parts. Part 1 discusses training in general and outlines different training skills and motivation strategies. Part 2 is a training plan for a HACCP course which contains both standard elements as well as recommendations for interactive exercises such as brainstorming sessions, discussions and workshops. You can decide for yourself which of the interactive elements you want to apply. However, if you take them all it may not be possible to fit them into the proposed schedule of a two-day course.

If you want to follow this guide *it means work*. You may find that lecturing about HACCP is far easier and less stressful than *communicating* HACCP – but this is the first step towards *doing* HACCP.

Good luck!

THE AUTHOR

Dagmar Engel graduated in biology from Cologne University in 1981 and has subsequently undertaken research work in immunology and held a post as a research assistant for a German television station. In addition, in her earlier career she had a number of teaching and training positions which varied from teaching biology to sixth formers to teaching music and dance to pre-school children.

Since the early 1990s she has worked internationally in the field of food safety both as a consultant and as a trainer. She has taught HACCP for several years in countries around the world to both members of industry and enforcement officials. She is the author and co-author of several books both in English and German, is a freelance journalist for a number of German magazines on the subjects of HACCP, food safety and training, and is a regularly invited speaker at international conferences.

The author may be contacted through the publishers.

CHAPTER 1

Introduction

The importance of understanding HACCP

During the last decade, the importance of food hygiene and HACCP has been increasingly acknowledged by both the food industry and official food control systems throughout the world. Since the implementation of the Food Hygiene Directive 93/43 in Europe HACCP has appeared in the headlines of countless magazines, industry guides and handbooks. Since the turn of the millennium, the HACCP concept – having come a long way since its primary application in space travel – should be a familiar term to every food-handler and its application in food processes self-evident. But is it really so?

When looking at HACCP systems it seems that there are obviously some mistakes which crop up regularly. Typical problems which prevent a HACCP concept from being effective are:

- the system is theoretically elaborated but not put into daily practice;

- the system is too abstract;

- the system lacks any connection to other internal concepts, e.g. hygiene management;

- the system has been developed at a senior company level but has never reached the staff on the work floor;

- people have not bothered to explain the system to those who actually have to work with it.

HACCP is a network system which needs thorough understanding from everybody. The fascination with HACCP has a lot to do with the fact that we cannot afford any of the usual 'caste systems' which exist in almost any business. Everybody's input and participation will influence the quality of the company's safety system: the newest recruit is as important in his or her behaviour as the most senior of managers. Like hygiene, HACCP needs total commitment. Commitment, however, needs motivation and motivation needs training.

Introducing the principles of HACCP needs time and sensitivity. A functioning safety concept cannot be created overnight. It will also depend upon existing preliminary measurements – the more you can rely upon, the easier the development of a process-specific concept will become. The same applies to the introduction of HACCP as a training subject – the more people know about hygiene principles the more easily will they become familiar with HACCP.

Why should you understand HACCP? Many things function without us having thorough knowledge of how they operate. Many people drive cars without having a clue how a combustion engine works. We use computers, enjoy TV programmes, listen to the radio and take advantage of any number of technical achievements without understanding the scientific background. In many cases this particular knowledge is not required: somebody who is in charge of temperature control in the cold storage units of a food company doesn't necessarily need to understand Carnot's theory of thermodynamics on which the principle of refrigeration is actually based. There is no doubt that you can train your staff how to check and measure physical, chemical or even microbiological parameters without explaining the meaning and intention of the HACCP concept, *but* getting into the depth of the HACCP philosophy will enhance everybody's attempts and efforts.

Familiarity with the HACCP concept means:

- knowing about product- and process-specific hazards;

- learning to estimate and assess individual risks;

- understanding why certain process steps are critical;

- understanding why certain criteria have to be observed;

- developing an individual judgement on how to deal with special situations, e.g. when criteria are not met and corrective actions are required.

The food hygiene regulations require every food handler to be trained and/or supervised. There is no explicit demand that this training – which will obviously encompass food hygiene principles – should also include HACCP. On the other hand, it will support the company's attitude towards due diligence if their staff are also trained in HACCP. For a manager of a food company it is compulsory to make sure that everybody who is entrusted with a certain task has the necessary know-how to deal with any possible situation associated with his or her job. In terms of food safety this will mean that people need to know which preventative measurements they have to observe and how these measurements will work in order to protect the customer. The additional knowledge of *why* all these steps are important will support people's motivation.

Motivation is the 'forgotten' ingredient of the HACCP concept. Besides theory and technology HACCP needs people. HACCP has been called both a philosophy and a tool (Mitchell, 1995), which means that it has to be both understood and applied.

Many recent problems with insufficient HACCP concepts are, however, caused by the fact that a lot of people are convinced that they know everything about HACCP – but in fact don't, or at least still have a long way to go. Many companies also follow the attitude that the staff 'do not need to not know about HACCP' as long as quality management can deal with it. They omit the fact that it is not the quality team who is in charge of product safety. At the end of the day everybody has to make his or her contribution – from the cleaning staff to the production manager. They all need to know about HACCP. And this is where we start.

Teaching HACCP – muddles 'n' misunderstandings

One advantage for English-speaking food handlers is the fact that the HACCP terminology is in English! Currently many European countries, e.g. Germany, France, Italy, etc. are struggling with the translation of HACCP terms into the food handler's native tongue, facing not only the problem of translating an English expression into their national language but also doing it in a way that it is understandable. False and ambiguous translations have already caused a lot of harm. However, this is not to say that many of the supposedly 'English' technical terms linked with the HACCP concept do not themselves need translation into 'everyday' English to facilitate a general understanding! This doesn't just mean explaining the difference between 'hazard' and 'risk' and clarifying expressions such as 'monitoring' or 'severity', but includes the numerous possible meanings of 'critical control point', to give but a few examples. Listed below are some typical problems when teaching HACCP.

Terminology and semantics

Explaining the classical HACCP terminology is like walking through a jungle of definitions, although a thorough understanding of the meaning of the HACCP definitions is essential for the success of any HACCP training programme. The problem is certainly not helped by the subtle differences in meaning between expressions such as 'verification', 'reviewing' and 'validation' (how much of a part do these terms actually play in the average food handler's jargon anyway?). Sometimes it may be worthwhile trying a training approach which dispenses with most of the 'sophisticated' terms but which focuses on the few definitions which are really needed.

A forest of decision trees

The tautological model of the decision tree to identify the critical control points has become very popular – in spite of its weaknesses (these will be discussed later). So popular has the model become that many HACCP experts have felt bound to modify, change or reinvent the decision tree all over again. The trainer now has a choice of any number of versions (unless he or she decides not to use the model at all).

HACCP – incompatible with small premises?

Since the implementation of the food hygiene regulations there have been many voices condemning HACCP as a concept for large premises only which can afford the extra staff to implement and maintain the system. There is some truth in this in so far as the origins of HACCP had a product-specific orientation which is most easily achieved and obtained by large manufacturing companies. However, the many individual approaches which the classical HACCP concept has evolved during the last decades should not be forgotten and there is no need for small premises and even one-man (or woman) companies to feel frustrated.

Documentation = frustration?

The principle of documentation, although quoted as among the seven HACCP principles of the Codex Alimentarius, is still contested as it is not explicitly mentioned in the European food hygiene directive. The amount of documentation which is necessary to prove that your system is functioning has to be considered in relation to the individual company. The more or less complete lack of official guidelines regarding documentation can lead to huge volumes of checklists which are both grotesque and unreal. The idea that 'HACCP is all about writing everything down' looms in many minds and represents a constant source of frustration.

Typical misunderstandings

Some typical misinterpretations that are to be frequently found are represented by the following quotations:

- 'Hand-washing is a CCP' (see also 'my apron is a critical control point').

  Wrong. Personal hygiene, cleaning concepts, pest management and waste disposal systems are, however, essential and important for the functioning of the HACCP concept, but they need to be established beforehand. Most of these wannabe CCPs cannot be controlled and monitored in an online procedure (which is one of the most crucial characteristics of a CCP). It is essential to make a clear distinction between hygiene preliminaries and HACCP elements. Although both will form a network in terms of a holistic hygiene management concept, the difference between hygiene modules and CCPs has to be understood.

- 'HACCP means quality' (see also 'our quality system will deal with HACCP as well').

    Careful. Although modern quality management and HACCP have a lot in common (both are preventative, proactive concepts), the target points are quite different. While quality management aims to satisfy the expectations of the consumer (which obviously means that, in line with changes in trends and consumer tastes etc., that aim is also subject to constant change) HACCP aims to guarantee a safe product (which is an absolute target). Typical quality features such as taste, smell, look, consistency, etc. are of less importance in the HACCP concept. It is true, however, that a company with a well functioning quality management may use part of the existing quality skeleton (especially in terms of documentation) to build up HACCP. But don't forget: while a food business can do without a quality system, it *cannot* do without HACCP principles.

- 'A typical hazard in food storage is the expiration of the "best-before/use-by" date.'

    Not quite right. While the expiration of a set date may be an indication that the product is no longer safe for use it is actually the potential multiplication of harmful micro-organisms which is the real hazard. An understanding of these relationships is essential to conduct a proper hazard analysis.

- 'A lot of CCPs means a lot of control.'

    Yes and no. While a lot of CCPs certainly means that a company has to involve *a lot* of time and manpower to carry out the necessary controls, it does not necessarily mean that they have an advantage over companies who manage with a minimum of CCPs. It is not the number of CCPs which will determine your safety level. After a close look you may find that many CCPs are not critical control points in the true sense of HACCP but may only involve quality criteria, hygiene elements or technical checkpoints.

- 'HACCP cannot be applied to small premises' (or alternatively 'HACCP cannot be applied to catering businesses').

    Wrong. Today's HACCP has many faces. There are even well functioning HACCP approaches for non-food items, e.g. cosmetics, and food packaging and food-related auxiliary items such as vending machines. HACCP is flexible – as long as you are prepared to leave the classic product-specific concept and follow other systems (e.g. assured-safe catering; process-specific concepts, etc.).

PART 1

Setting Up a Training Course in HACCP

CHAPTER 2

Hygiene Training – The Classic Problems

The standard of food hygiene is influenced by the general layout and structure of premises, the design and maintenance of equipment and utensils, and the efficiency of cleaning concepts and temperature controls, but it is influenced most of all by people and their actions. The best equipment cannot protect a company from the damage caused by food contamination if the food handlers are not aware of their own personal responsibilities. This means that food hygiene training is an essential stepping stone on the way towards food safety.

Why do we need training in hygiene?

Obviously the major aim of food hygiene training is the prevention of food contamination and food poisoning outbreaks. Food hygiene training is also a demonstration of due diligence as it serves to reassure both customers and the food safety authorities.

Training in general means 'bringing a person to a desired standard of efficiency' (Oxford English Dictionary). Training needs to be carried out by means of both instruction and practice. This means that both theory and practice play an important part in the education of food handlers. Theory means some knowledge about the facts leading to food contamination (food microbiology, storage pests, chemical and physical hazards, etc.), but also about techniques like temperature control, cleaning and disinfection, food preservation and the practical application of HACCP principles.

Only too often the practical part is left out – either because training is delivered as a 'one-off event' without regard to the situation on the work-floor or because training does not take into consideration that every theory needs to be applied, or at least put into a practical demonstration, in order to be thoroughly understood.

Food handlers are usually adult persons who will bring their own experiences, expectations and frustrations into the training situation. Most of them will have a pre-set personal attitude towards hygiene which will influence their convictions. To some extent one's attitude towards hygiene depends on individual sources, e.g. family, school, friends and personal experience:

- *Family experience.* Some families pay a lot of attention to cleanliness and 'proper' appearance. Children are taught to wash and bathe regularly, have clean fingernails and wear neat clothes whereas in other families hygiene does not necessarily play an important part in family life.

- *School.* There is no reason why hygiene should not be taught at school (bearing in mind that approximately 50% of all food poisoning is caused by private households or non-professionals). Hygiene can be a fascinating school subject encompassing both personal hygiene as well as food hygiene strategies. It is quite surprising how much influence school experiences have on your professional life. If hygiene has never been an issue during primary or secondary school it will be more difficult to show and explain its importance during the professional learning experience.

- *Friends.* The kind of attitude which is demonstrated by close friends is often 'trend-setting'. Some youth groups pride themselves in being demonstratively scruffy or grotty whereas other youngsters take great interest in body care and a well-groomed appearance.

- *Personal experience.* 'Once bitten, twice shy' – somebody who has already experienced severe food poisoning symptoms will not want to go through such an ordeal again. Additionally, the media may play an important part in raising an individual's awareness: with food poisoning outbreaks, chemical contamination of foods and new food-borne diseases (BSE, VTEC, etc.) filling the daily headlines a personal interest in such matters is easily raised and maintained.

What are the problems in hygiene training?

This background is further formed by professional development, professional experience, observation and on-the-job training. This is often where the problems start.

Problem 1: The subject of hygiene is neglected during professional training

A food handler is supposed to have received thorough training in his or her craft (butchering, baking, catering, selling, etc.). This does not necessarily include a thorough knowledge of good hygiene practices.

Problem 2: Hygiene is taught without practical reference

Even where hygiene has been on the curriculum, future food handlers may well have learned a lot about 'germs' and 'toxins' but do not see the link to their daily kitchen practices.

Problem 3: Hygiene is a matter of interpretation

The success of training also depends considerably on the company's attitude. Hygiene rules need to be supported by the management, which means that the essential framework for the implementation and enforcement of hygiene rules need to be in place Sometimes hygiene seems to be a subject of interpretation and is not taken seriously enough.

Problem 4: Hygiene yes – enforcement no

Sometimes the enforcement of hygiene rules is a little dubious. If hygiene rules are not supported by the basic preliminaries of implementation, e.g. proper protective clothing, satisfactory facilities for hand washing, etc., staff will lose their faith in them.

Problem 5: No feedback is given

Motivation and feedback are essential for the maintenance of hygiene rules: the staff must feel that following good hygiene practices is also of a personal benefit because their efforts are acknowledged by the management.

What are the consequences of poor hygiene training?

This list above is not claimed to be exhaustive. Typical staff problems which usually result as a consequence of 'shaky' hygiene concepts are as follows:

- The enforcement of hygiene rules is not complete. Personal hygiene rules should be the same for everybody. If supervisors, external service engineers, important clients, etc. are permitted to enter the premises without obeying the general hygiene rules staff motivation with continuously decrease. The management's attitude has to be exemplary. Often there is a lack of supporting provisions: there may be not enough lockers for the staff to store their professional items; empty soap dispensers are never refilled in time, etc.

- Ideas arise such as 'traditional practice' (giving rise to such comments as 'my grandfather never wore protective head gear and nobody ever got poisoned' or 'we have always done it like this, and nothing bad has ever happened') and 'misdemeanour attitudes' become prevalent ('why is it so important to wash and disinfect my hands regularly if I can do three cream gateaux during the same time and help my company's turnover?'). Newly introduced protective clothing is often looked upon as an unnecessary 'masquerade' – especially if the management does not act as an example.

- Hygiene rules are set up to be obeyed like orders without the necessary information about the reasons why these rules are important for everybody. Without thorough explanation they may be obeyed but will never be understood.

Why do we need to consider the basics?

Why is it so important to have a close look at staff hygiene? Because your HACCP training will never work without these essential preliminaries. Just as any HACCP concept set up without due attention to the basic hygiene requirements is doomed to become an abstract and lifeless paper exercise, HACCP training may be of theoretical interest but will never be fully understood let alone put into daily practice by those who are not convinced of the importance of good hygiene practices. Before starting to teach HACCP a thorough assessment of the individual 'hygiene background' of your trainees is essential.

CHAPTER 3

Motivation – An Important Training Tool

Motivation is a tool – for both trainer and trainee. To ensure the success of your training you need to be able not only to give a good presentation but also to provide general encouragement for 'why HACCP is important for everybody'. In fact there is no good presentation without motivation.

Encouraging motivation

Self-motivation comes first. If the trainer has no self-motivation, he or she will not be able to motivate others. It is also difficult to remain motivated if your delegates appear tired, passive, stubborn or even negative. In such circumstances you have to draw on your inner resources. In fact the most important skills for a professional trainer to demonstrate are:

- relaxation;

- inner strength/power;

- flexibility.

When dealing with non-responsive delegates try to adopt the following attitude:

Everybody has got all the necessary potential to lead a successful life, overcome difficulties and change unfavourable situations. Equally, everybody has good and bad traits. It makes much more sense to use their positive capacities than to try to fight and suppress their bad attributes.

HACCP can be looked at as a network. If a net has 99 good knots but one is torn, the whole net is useless. Part of everybody's motivation should be that, at the end of the day, it is their choice if they want to be a firm knot or a hole . . .

To help you, below are suggested some methods for encouraging motivation:

- *Acknowledge established know-how.* Link into the trainees' professional work experience. Everybody is an expert in his or her own field. The experience that trainees bring with them should be acknowledged and used.

- *Give credit where it is due.* Helpful contributions should be appreciated. Adults lack confidence in their abilities as learners. *But* do not over-praise!

- *Establish connections to familiar situations.* Link the subject of HACCP to situations in their private lives such as kitchen and household practices as well as personal experiences in terms of personal hygiene. Bring everybody into the picture: what can happen in a food business can be of consequence to you, your partner, your children.

- *Be provocative!* Sometimes provocation is the only solution in situations where delegates get obstinate, negative or tired. Provocation stirs and keeps people awake. Use 'neutral' formulations such as 'What would you think of somebody who . . .' or 'Would you go and buy food knowing that . . .' The message that everybody is a customer at the end of the day can prove to be helpful.

- *Establish 'in-house' patterns.* This is a good motivation method for in-house training sessions. The trainer could start sentences with: 'In this company we will . . .' or 'Our company policy will be . . .' This will establish a corporate identity in terms of hygiene practices. The company's HACCP system will be as good as the team who supports it – and every team is only as good as its weakest member.

Motivation needs to be kept alive during the whole seminar (and certainly beyond!). Training is like starting an engine. To keep it going further energy has to be applied. A good trainer should leave enough motivation behind to keep the HACCP machinery in working order.

Skills and attributes required by trainers

Every training situation involves a trainer and somebody who is to be trained – in the classic situation usually one trainer and a varying number of delegates. The trainer has at least one advantage: usually he or she has also been on the other side of the fence and, like every trainee, will remember both encouraging and disappointing learning situations. A professional trainer is to a certain extent responsible for the success of the course. Success will also depend on the interactions between the group members but a good trainer should be able to influence and steer this aspect.

There are certain attributes a trainer should have as well as the appropriate skills to enable him or her to establish a good working relationship with trainees to get the best out of them:

- personality

- clear diction

- communication

- credibility

- knowledge of subject.

Equally important is a positive approach to the subject and the way you introduce the topic will be picked up by the delegates. Negative projections will provoke negative responses and your trainees' willingness to learn will decrease. A positive approach –

'Today we're going to learn how we can master the problem of cross-contamination' – will create good feelings and help in situations of stress. You can either 'sell' training as a dour 'must' or promote it as a wonderful opportunity to get more information about the background behind obviously essential rules. For most trainees the training situation is an exceptional one which takes them out of the daily working routine – a good trainer can make this experience a very exciting one which they will want to repeat or a chore which will make them glad when it's finally over.

There are also some techniques which are required by a good trainer. They include the following:

- *The ability to communicate.* There is a difference between lecturing and training. Lecturing is a monologue – training is dialogue. A good trainer *talks and listens* to people, answers questions, perhaps raising questions on his or her own behalf. Being communicative means being interested in your trainees.

- *The ability to socialise.* Some training courses will have a very mixed audience. Particularly when small or medium-sized premises are involved you will have every possible staff level from the manager down to the casual worker. In other courses you may find people who may hardly ever work together or people who are usually in awe of one another sitting next to each other. The secret is to create a common understanding among the delegates, find a language that everybody can follow and make them aware that in terms of hygiene they are all in the same boat.

- *The ability to encourage.* 'This is not possible', 'this won't work', 'our premises are not up to it' – these or similar killer phrases are quite familiar in the training business. Challenge your delegates. 'Does that mean that *you* are not able to do/understand/follow these ideas?', 'somebody like you will certainly know a way to find a solution to these problems', and so. Your comments should not be presented in a patronising way, but encourage your trainees to find their own answers. Individual solutions mean 'ownership' – 'this is *my* way'. However, bear in mind that:

  – solutions need time;

–   you may have to be patient and accept communication 'breaks';

–   your 'advices' are just that – 'vices'. They prevent the trainees from finding their own solutions

Trainers also need to follow a few basic rules::

- be responsible for yourself;

- express yourself clearly;

- bear in mind that different people may have different opinions;

- have fun!

Below is a short checklist for trainers as group leaders:

- How do you see yourself in relation to the delegates? (As teacher, professor, scientific expert, coach, buddy?)

- How will the group see you? (Not necessarily as you see yourself!)

- How much do you want to involve the group? (Is this going to be a one-person-performance or a joint attempt?)

- How flexible are you? (Can you change the subject if necessary? Can you provide additional information on subjects of particular interest? How much time will you give the delegates to answer a question before you answer it for them?)

The size of the class (see below) is of crucial importance for developing the course as the number of delegates will decide the most suitable presentation technique to use. For the purpose of HACCP training it is recommended that you set a limit of 12 delegates per group, this being the ideal group size. Indeed, when training an in-house HACCP team you will rarely get more than this number. The situation may be different, however, if you are offering HACCP management seminars as open learning courses or are giving a basic introduction to HACCP for an entire production staff.

(This last case would not be regarded as HACCP training as it is usually an extension of the staff's hygiene training.)

What about the trainees?

It is important that you have as much background information on your trainees as possible.

How much do you know about the delegates?

There are certain elements of HACCP training which can be presented as a standardised package, but it will always be useful if you are able to adjust the subject to match the individual circumstances of your delegates. This will earn you more credibility than you would receive by 'churning out' non-specific programmes which do not take into consideration that different premises may require different information and details.

How much do you know about the educational background of your delegates? How can you find out? Bear in mind that this information will help you to adjust your level of language and approach to suit your audience.

How do you make them feel comfortable?

For most of your delegates the training situation will mean a change from the daily routine, sometimes a pleasant diversion, sometimes unwanted stress. Your opening remarks can create an atmosphere which is either relaxed or strained. Take your time and watch the group. Are they relaxed among themselves? Sometimes a group will consist of colleagues who may never actually meet on a day-to-day basis, and this might create an atmosphere of awkwardness. Your task is to loosen everybody up – in a stressed situation you will not get the feedback you want. The perfect atmosphere should be one of trust and respect.

What rules do you set for the group?

To guarantee smooth progress in the training certain basic rules have to be obeyed. These rules may vary depending on the composition of the group. Sometimes you may tolerate a free discussion; at other times it may be necessary to ask the delegates to raise their hands when they want to contribute.

There are other basic rules which may help both trainer and the course. Examples are a 'no smoking' policy for the duration of the course and, equally importantly, the requirement to 'switch off all pagers/mobile phones etc.'. However, whatever rules you set for the group you must also follow yourself.

Finally, don't forget – all rules should be agreed at the beginning of the course!

CHAPTER 4

Preparing the Course

Every training course is based on elementary modules which need to be thoroughly prepared. These 'basics' are listed below:

- the environment

- the content

- the teaching methods

- the resources

- the course evaluation.

In terms of the training course itself there are two possible scenarios:

- the selected circle – the trainer invites a selected group, usually to a venue chosen by the trainer;

- the given circle – a client employs the trainer to train a given number of staff members, usually at a venue provided by the customer.

These are obviously two different starting points. In the first case the trainer not only has a set programme but is also familiar with the training environment; in the second case the trainer needs to adjust the programme to meet the needs of the delegates and the given situation.

The course environment

The environment means much more just than the classroom. There are a number of factors which will have an influence on the atmosphere of the course:

- light

- air

- temperature

- space

- time

- noise

- media employed.

Sometimes the trainer may be able to choose the training environment but on other occasions he or she will be confronted with conditions which leave few possibilities for alteration.

The sections which follow provide a brief checklist of aspects to consider regarding the environment.

Does the environment suit the atmosphere you are trying to create?

Usually the trainer will prefer a rather 'neutral' environment and most training or conference rooms match this expectation. Problems arise when a company which cannot provide training facilities of its own hires a room. Many trainers have to perform in the back room of a restaurant, in a clubroom or even in a gym. You can well imagine that a room stuffed with paintings, trophies and other decorations will not help you to attract the full attention of the delegates.

Is the room the right size?

If the room is too small, the delegates will feel cramped and restricted in their personal space. On the other hand, if the room is too large they will simply feel lost. Both circumstances will make them feel uncomfortable.

Are there facilities to black out the room, to use electrical equipment, etc?

This will certainly depend on the training media you intend to use, but usually you will need at least one power point. When using slides, acetates in overhead projectors, etc. you will need a projection screen and you will need to be able to dim the lights.

What do you need to provide yourself?

A professional trainer usually has a questionnaire for the client to answer in order to make sure that all necessary media are in place. Usually you will need something to write on (e.g. blackboard, flip-chart, etc.) and probably at least one electronic device (overhead projector, slide projector, TV and VCR for videos, etc.) You will also need a screen or at least a white, empty wall for projections. Pinboard systems with coloured moderation sheets are very useful in workshop and presentation situations but may present a transport problem. Make sure it is clear with the client who is to supply the training aids.

Are you free to arrange the furniture?

The way you seat your delegates can make a big difference. Open arrangements (semi-circle, horse-shoe, etc.) will enable the trainer to join the delegates' circle and also allow some room for movement around the room. Closed arrangements (e.g. rows) will isolate the trainer from the group. For the purpose of workshop situations it may be important to be able to change the furniture, i.e. create several large working tables.

The course content

A good training programme is based on modules. We will talk about the structure of the HACCP seminar later on in detail, but as HACCP is based on hygiene most courses cannot plunge into the subject without addressing a few hygiene topics to make sure that the necessary basic knowledge is understood. The subjects listed below are elementary food hygiene modules and should be addressed at every training level:

- basic food microbiology;

- food poisoning and food contamination and its prevention;

- basic hazard analysis;

- personal hygiene rules;

- good hygiene practices;

- premise hygiene and pest prevention;

- cleaning and disinfection;

- due diligence.

Checklist for course content

- *Do you have clear aims and objectives?* What are you going to teach and what do you expect the delegates to learn from the course?

- *Are you being realistic about how much you can achieve?* Time, the receptivity of the delegates, the complexity of the subject, etc. are factors which may put a limit on what you can get across. Don't forget that you are the one who is familiar with the subject – it may be completely new to your trainees.

- *Does the content follow a logical sequence?* Subjects like hazard analysis and risk assessment will appear much clearer if they follow a short lecture brushing up the (hopefully) existing knowledge on basic food microbiology, chemical hazards and physical contamination. Equally, the principle of monitoring will only be understood, when people are familiar with microbiological, chemical and physical parameters.

- *Does the content take into account what people already know?* Making assumptions like 'I'm sure you all know everything about HACCP' or 'I don't think we need to talk about bacteria' is always dangerous. It is usually worthwhile holding a brief 'question and answer session' at the beginning of every training session to assess the existing knowledge and the gaps that need to be filled. It is important to encourage the trainees because a lot of them may not want to admit their lack of knowledge about a subject. Tell them that this is their big chance – today they can ask all the questions that nobody has answered for them so far.

Teaching methods – principles and purposes

Training is hard work, because not only do you have to win the attention of your trainees but you have to get them ready to follow you through your performance. The easier you make it for them the more likely it is that you will succeed. We have already mentioned the techniques and skills required by a good trainer. They also include the following abilities:

- to convert academic jargon into simple everyday language (why use the expression 'bacterial toxins' if 'poisons formed by bacteria' explains it far better?);

- to establish and maintain trainees' attention;

- to present new and up-to-date information;

- to talk without distracting mannerisms (verbally and physically: try to avoid 'big gestures' – eye-to-eye contact is far more important!).

Teaching needs to relate to the circumstances on the shop floor. The trainees need to be able to picture themselves in the situation, and case studies (see below) are a good tool to use to help achieve this. Try to be as practical as possible. Always put theoretical facts across in relation to what happens in the kitchen (the bakery, the retail shop, the meat processing plant, etc.).

Teaching methods have to take into consideration the memory retention curve of the trainees which takes the pattern shown in Table 4.1.

Table 4.1 Amount of information retained after various activities

Learning technique	Memory retention
Read	10%
Hear	20%
See	30%
Hear and see	50%
Discuss	70%
Do	90%

Depending on the subject and the time available there are different methods of presentation. Each one has its advantages and disadvantages. We will look here at the following methods:

- the lecture;

- the demonstration;

- the case study;

- the discussion.

Method 1: Lecture/performance

A lecture is the presentation of a subject by one person. It can additionally contain personal statements, comments and recommendations. The lecturer takes on an active role whereas the trainee is rather passive (listening, eventually taking notes). Lecturing is ideal for abstract and scientific subjects, and can be the basis for other methods, e.g. discussion.

Method 1: Lecture

Advantages	• Best method to transmit a lot of ideas to be learned in a relatively short time
	• Easy to prepare in advance
	• Time and subject can be thoroughly planned
Disadvantages	• Apart from non-verbal communication (facial expressions, body language) the lecturer gets hardly any feedback
	• Without feedback it is difficult to adjust the lecturing speed – some trainees may not be able to follow
	• Without any breaks the trainees have no time to gather and formulate individual thoughts
	• Memory retention is reduced
How to do it	• Speak as freely as possible
	• Establish and hold eye contact
	• Check and train your control of language (long sentences often result in muddled grammar and sense)
	• Take a break every now and then to promote active thinking
	• Be positive and humorous
	• Start by giving a synopsis of your lecture

Method 2: Demonstration

When demonstrating a subject the trainer imitates a real situation by using demonstration objects or other materials like videotapes. The aim is either to show how to use certain tools or demonstrate a situation which requires active input. This method can be employed to visualise processes and to provide training in recognising actions and connections.

Method 2: Demonstration	
Advantages	• The subject is experienced by hearing and seeing • Supports the learning process more than the 'trial and error' method • Memory retention is increased • Explanation of the subject is easier
Disadvantages	• Preparation of a demonstration requires time and effort • The maximum number of trainees is reduced • The trainees' activities are restricted to passive watching • Independent thinking is not encouraged
How to do it	• Prepare your resources: room, utensils, demonstration objects • Capture and control the trainees' attention by focusing on special points or steps in your demonstration • Let them evaluate and discuss what they have seen and heard

Method 3: Case study/workshop

This is more a learning than a teaching method as it encourages input from the trainees: not only do they have to speak about a problem but they have to validate the circumstances and present and discuss solutions.

A case study can be practised as a 'critical incident analysis' (CIA). The analysis should follow the classic 'Sherlock Holmes' type questions:

• *Who* was involved?

• *Where* did it happen?

• *When* did it happen?

- *Why* did it happen?

- *How* could it happen?

This is an effective method for looking at potential problems in a workshop situation. Active discussion supports the application of results and solutions to similar incidents which may occur daily in a real-life situation. The learning process does not depend on abstract facts but is facilitated by personal engagement. Analysing critical incidents can help to:

- identify warning signs;

- explore causes and sources of incidents;

- create general policies or practices for managing potentially disruptive incidents (or for capitalising on fortunate incidents).

A special form of case study is the 'mock trial' exercise: the trainees imitate a court case (e.g. an outbreak of food-poisoning) where they provide the prosecution and defence using fictional evidence.

Method 3: Case study/workshop	
Advantages	• The trainee does not get stuck in the usual conjectural 'I would think that . . .' but can identify with the situation
	• This method concentrates on facts and causative factors
	• The workshop exercise promotes independent thinking and sensibility thus encouraging the trainees' cognitive abilities
Disadvantages	• If the case material is unrealistic, or the solution is too difficult or too easy, the value of the exercise is questionable
	• Some trainees may 'over-identify' with the case which may lead to tensions in the group

	• Workshop groups have to be small to involve everybody
How to do it	• Set your aims clearly • Support the presentation of the case with written materials, newspaper articles, videos, etc. • Set a time limit • As soon as the workshop has started your input should be reduced to the occasional comment • If possible ask the group for more than one way of solving the case – these proposals can then be compared, contrasted and validated

Method 4: Discussion

The 'open forum' discussion has no hierarchy: all participants are equal and have the same right to contribute. The method is intended to promote individual contribution and to encourage participation from all intellectual abilities. A special form of the open discussion is the brainstorming session which is meant to encourage the trainees' creativity, although all discussion methods support the association of ideas and the finding of solutions. For a brainstorming session, the discussion 'climate' should be unconstrained and 'easy' to allow everyone to contribute, however far-fetched their ideas, and every input is equally valid.

Method 4: Discussion	
Advantages	• Keeps trainees active and therefore awake • Encourages trainees to find their own solutions • Individual solutions mean 'ownership' • Encourages group communication and general understanding

Disadvantages	• Discussion methods require a lot of time
	• Without tutoring there is a danger that discussions can degenerate into dispute
	• Discussions can always take unexpected turns or wander off the point
	• Weak and timid group members may be cut short
How to do it	• Name a problem, but don't give any ideas for the solution
	• All ideas should be collected (e.g. written on a blackboard)
	• The 'brainstorming' method only asks for ideas, *not* for comments!
	• If necessary, set some rules, e.g. asking for speaking permission, limiting speaking time, etc.
	• Encourage shy group members to contribute – use the 'everybody has to give us at least one idea' tactic

Checklist for the trainer on teaching methods

• Are you familiar with the advantages and disadvantages of the different teaching methods?

• How do you involve the group?

• Do your teaching methods allow the sharing of knowledge?

• Do you vary your methods?

Resources – tools, aids, support

Preparing a subject means designing a programme. Your decision about *how* the training should be done is equally important. Preparation of the subject usually entails three different stages:

- the collection of materials/facts;

- compression of the contents;

- visualising the subject.

There are many different ways to present a subject as we have seen above: you can talk about it, discuss it and demonstrate it. The last method may involve visual aids such as:

- overhead projector;

- flipchart/pinboard;

- slide projector;

- computer software (e.g. Microsoft PowerPoint presentations);

- videos;

- equipment for carrying out experiments.

All of these aids will require preparation *and* facilities which need to be available, booked in advance if necessary (unless you provide them yourself) and working (!).

You should recognise that there is a certain danger in using too many different resources as people may become sidetracked by method of presentation rather than concentrate on the message. A combination of overhead projector, flipchart and pinboard for workshop situations is ideal and quite sufficient for the purposes of a HACCP seminar. Slides should only be used to show working situations (both good and bad examples). Videos should be kept short – a maximum of 12 minutes is ideal.

Checklist for resources

- Have you previewed your material?

- If resources have to be shared (e.g. handouts, case studies, questionnaires), have you prepared enough for everyone?

- Are you familiar with the training aids? Do you know how to work/switch on the equipment? Would you be able to sort out technical problems?

Summary

To be successful HACCP courses need to be interactive. The more the delegates become actively involved the more they will retain. A good course should be beneficial to both delegates and trainer as both can learn from each other. This will only be possible if both parties work together.

CHAPTER 5

Structuring the Course

To set up an efficient course programme you will need to structure the course. The course structure needs to have regard to:

- the course contents;

- the training methods;

- the training media;

- the time schedule.

Lectures, workshops and presentations should alternate with each other to keep the trainees attentive. Your lectures should be separated by interactive sessions to which every trainee can contribute. The more your trainees work out for themselves the more they will retain.

Basic course structure

Below is a possible structure for a basic course entitled 'Introduction to HACCP':

Part 1 Introduction

Food safety – what does it mean?

Food safety control measures

HACCP – what does it mean?

The history of HACCP

What's new?

Part 2 Definitions

What is the meaning of:

–   Hazard

–   Risk

–   Hazard analysis and risk assessment

–   Monitoring

–   Verification

Part 3 Setting up a HACCP system

The seven principles

HACCP in 12 steps

Part 4 HACCP for different food industries

Manufacturers

Retailers

Caterers

Transport businesses

Part 5 Maintaining the HACCP system

Documentation

Reviewing

Auditing

Part 6 HACCP and your hygiene concept

Hygiene preliminaries

Hygiene responsibilities

Quality concepts

Interactive workshops can be held in any part of the course. The duration of the course could be either two full days (intensive HACCP training) or six sessions spread over a given amount of time.

This course could be held as a general introduction to HACCP for food handlers, supervisors, service personnel, food hygiene consultants and environmental health officers (EHOs). When training a specific branch of the food industry you may want to adapt Part 4 to the special needs of your trainees. It may, however, be useful to teach the full course in order to draw a comparison between different kinds of businesses.

Training media required

The training media required are:

- a flipchart (alternatively a blackboard);

- an overhead projector (and overhead acetates);

- a pinboard.

Optional training aids, depending on your resources, would include:

- slide projector and slides;

- videos.

Feedback and certification

Feedback from successful participation can be provided by:

- active participation and presentation in a workshop situation;

- written tests;

- written assignments (e.g. trainees conduct a HACCP analysis on a chosen subject/product).

What kind of certificate will be issued will depend on the purpose and intention of both the course and the client. There are, indeed, many standardised HACCP training courses available from different British training institutions, e.g.

- the Chartered Institute of Environmental Health;

- the Royal Environmental Health Institute of Scotland;

- the Royal Society of Public Health and Hygiene;

- the Royal Society of Health.

You may find that the general skeleton of these courses is actually quite similar, but the examinations necessary to qualify for the course certificate may well be different.

Conclusion

The following chapters describe different approaches to the delivery of the course subjects. The intention of the course is to provide the trainees with sufficient skills to begin and maintain the implementation of HACCP principles in their own company.

PART 2

Teaching a Training Course in HACCP

CHAPTER 6

Teaching HACCP – Introducing the Subject

All training – whether it's physical exercise or theoretical education – should start with a 'warm-up'. 'Warming up' in this context means tuning into the subject and making your trainees familiar with what you are going to tell them. Most trainees attending a HACCP course have probably gone through some basic food hygiene training and know the elementary principles. The trainer should, however, assess the existing knowledge of the class. This can take place as part of the general personal introduction – 'Tell us your name, and say something about yourself and your function in your company. What are your previous experiences with food hygiene in general and HACCP in particular? What makes you attend this course?' People should be encouraged to admit that they do not know a great deal about HACCP and are about to start 'from scratch'. However, any experience that trainees bring to the course should be acknowledged and, if possible, used.

Step 1: The meaning of food safety

The first part of your introduction to HACCP could take the form of a question and answer session:

- *Why* do we need procedures to make food safe – or to make safe food?

- *What* are the common/traditional methods to achieve food safety?

- *Who* is to be protected?

- *What* happens without food safety?

- *What* are some examples of food safety control measures?

Key terms to get across are:

- food poisoning;

- food contamination;

- consumer protection;

- internal control measures (e.g. temperature controls, hygiene practices);

- external controls (e.g. food surveillance systems).

Step 2: A short history of food safety

This topic could be covered by means of a lecture to get across the following sort of information.

Knowledge of food poisoning and food contamination is very old. In fact, Hygieia was the Greek goddess of health (the link with our term 'hygiene' is clear), and the idea of 'clean' and 'unclean' foods is to be found in many of the world's religions. We even find early rules for the preparation of food in the Old Testament. (*Note for the trainer:* do some research for interesting examples!) The arbitrary contamination or adulteration of food was seriously punished so we may conclude that man has always been concerned to keep food wholesome.

However, there were very few ways to find out whether food was contaminated and whatever methods were available were complicated.

Step 3: Explain the term HACCP

Explain the letters H A C C P. Key concepts to include are:

- hazard;

- hazard analysis;

- control;

- control point;

- critical control point.

Note for the trainer

This exercise could be carried out as a question and answer session.

Step 4: The evolution of HACCP

Again this could be explained by means of a lecture along the following lines:

- relate the development of the HACCP concept by NASA and Pillsbury whose intention was to create a proactive control system;

- explain the use of HACCP in the USA;

- outline HACCP in European legislation;

- discuss the relationship between HACCP and the World Health Organisation;

- introduce the Food Hygiene Regulations 1995;

- discuss HACCP today.

Note for the trainer

This is not meant to be an extensive lecture but an explanation of the background behind why it was necessary to develop a proactive system and its increasing importance.

Step 5: What's new?

The aims and objectives of this part of the introduction are to compare traditional reactive food safety systems with HACCP, pointing out the benefits of a proactive concept involving all staff members.

Key concepts to include are:

- chemical and microbiological food sampling;

- laboratory tests;

- costs of external expertise;

- typical parameters to control;

- on-line control measurements;

- prediction of potential hazards;

- direct involvement of staff;

- network control systems.

Conclusion

This first session is meant to introduce HACCP. The steps described above will help the trainees to learn that the idea of food safety systems is not new at all, and HACCP can be seen as a modern tool to achieve the production of safe food. Trainers who like pithy aphorisms to sum up the subject are recommended to use the quotation from Mitchell (1995):

> In principle HACCP is a philosophy. In practice it is a tool.

Let your students discuss the meaning.

CHAPTER 7

'Talking HACCP'– Bringing Sense into the Definitions

This session is all about understanding. HACCP may be regarded as a tool, and the use of any tool requires at least some technological knowledge. When you drive a car you have to be familiar with terms like engine, brakes, accelerator, shock-absorber, exhaust, etc. Other and different technical terms will be found for kitchen utensils, electronic devices or cleaning equipment. Like every tool HACCP has its own language, and to understand it thoroughly it is necessary to explain a number of terms.

The aims and objectives of this session, therefore, are to define and explain the following terms:

- hazard;

- risk;

- severity;

- hazard analysis;

- risk assessment;

- CCP;

- monitoring;

- verification.

Step 1: Hazard, risk, severity

The first part of this session could take the form of a brainstorming session to determine what is:

- a general hazard;

- a food hazard.

Ask the trainees to list as many hazards as they can come up with. This can best e achieved using a 'pinboard' – every idea/statement is put on a slip of paper and pinned to a demonstration chart. This allows the 'hazards' to be organised into groups after everybody has contributed.

The objective of the exercise is to

- to make clear that hazards are factors or agents, not circumstances;

- to differentiate between biological, chemical and physical hazards;

- to differentiate between serious hazards (i.e. pathogens) and mere annoyances (i.e. a fly in the soup).

A recommended approach is to work towards the following definition:

> A hazard is anything – microbiological, chemical, physical – that might cause harm to a consumer.

It is also necessary to make clear that in terms of HACCP the person to be protected is the consumer, not the food handler, although in some cases they may be the same person.

In order to discuss the seriousness of different hazards the term 'severity' should be introduced using the definition by Bryan (1992):

> Severity is the magnitude of the hazard or the seriousness of possible consequence.

Following on from this you could perhaps set up a question and answer session to explain the difference between hazard and risk. The key terms and concepts to include here would be:

- probability;

- likelihood;

- estimation;

- influence.

The objective at this point is to point out that:

- hazards are absolute;

- risks are relative and can be influenced;

- actual risk = probability $\times$ severity.

Note for the trainer

To explain the relationship between hazard and risk you could use the 'jungle scenario'(see MacDonald and Engel, 1996):

Imagine yourself in a jungle. There is certainly a large number of hazards you could experience – some of them really serious such as wild beasts of prey, others perhaps not quite so threatening like insect bites. Your greatest possible hazard could be a hungry tiger, a venomous snake or a crocodile which is threatening your life. Depending on the kind of jungle you're in, the *probability* of these hazards occurring may vary greatly. For example, the risk of encountering a tiger in Malaysia is certainly much greater than the risk of becoming a tiger's lunch in the Scottish Highlands. Your personal behaviour and the *protective measurements* you take are also of importance – the risk of being bitten by a snake will obviously be reduced by wearing a pair of strong boots. In addition your path through the jungle has to be taken into account – if you walk along a river the likelihood of meeting one or two crocodiles is much greater than it would be if you took a different path far away from any water.

Of course not all hazards are equally dangerous. Some hazards are life-threatening while others can cause illness or discomfort. You could find that if a crocodile bites your leg off it may well be rather dangerous and extremely painful but your life, although not your limb, can be saved by quick reactions and adequate treatment. On the other hand, the bite of a small snake, though perhaps less painful or remarkable at first sight, could lead to death in a very short time.

This brings us to the term *severity*.

Step 2: Hazard analysis and risk assessment

The aims and objectives of this section are to explain the basis of hazard analysis. To achieve this the definitions of Step 1 can be used to show that hazards can be:

- product specific;

- process specific.

To get this point across compare the hazards associated with:

- different products (i.e. fruit/vegetables and fish);

- different processes (i.e. cooking and freezing).

Note for the trainer

If you have enough time divide the trainees into two groups to discuss products and processes and compare the examples which arise. For each product and process discuss:

- common hazards; and

- specific hazards.

Point out again that hazard analysis is to be considered from the customer's point of view.

To assess the actual risk of a hazard occuring (*risk assessment*) more factors have to be taken into account and estimated. Key terms and concepts to introduce are:

- likelihood;

- effects on health;

- severity;

- imminent risks;

- exposure;

- age/health status;

- high and low risk products.

The trainees should be brought to the following conclusions:

- that *hazard analysis* means the identification of potential hazards;

- that *risk assessment* is a method of estimating the likelihood of a hazard occurring *and* its severity if it should occur.

Step 3: Critical control points

The concept of the critical control point (CCP) is fundamental to the HACCP system and most trainees will have already heard the term. However, before going into details it is worthwhile holding a brief question and answer session to collect different explanations and ideas about the meaning of 'CCP':

- What is a CCP?

- What does 'control' mean?

- What is 'critical'?

- What makes a control point a 'critical' control point?

Key concepts to include in the discussion are:

- control measurements;

- elimination/reduction of hazards;

- unacceptable risks.

Note for the trainer

Below are some suggestions the trainer may find useful at this point:

- Introduce/discuss different 'official' definitions of the term 'CCP' (from the ICMSF, WHO, Codex, etc.).

- Introduce and discuss the difference between CCP 1 (elimination of a hazard) and CCP 2 (controlling/reducing a hazard).

- Chose a typical CCP (i.e. a heating process) and let the trainees discuss the following key words: criteria, preventative measurements, control measurements.

Note that the semantic distinction between 'CCP 1' and 'CCP 2' should only be made if it helps the course or if the company intends to use these expressions.

You may decide at this point to introduce the 'decision tree' to identify critical control points although we recommend discussion of this is left until the next session.

Step 4: Monitoring

You have identified a CCP. You could perhaps hold a question and answer session to discuss what happens next. Key terms and concepts to introduce are:

- parameters/criteria;

- observation;

- measurement;

- recording;

- deviation;

- alert systems;

- out-of-control situations.

The objective at this point is to point out that:

- different parameters require different monitoring procedures;

- there are differences between online and offline controls.

Note for the trainer

You may wish to introduce the term 'corrective action' as the concept is closely related.

Step 5: Verification

While the principle of verification will be explained and discussed in detail at a later stage it is often necessary to introduce the term much earlier. A popular synonym is 'reviewing'. Discuss its meaning.

Note for the trainer

Some suggestions for ways to tackle this are given below:

- Introduce/discuss different 'official' definitions of the term 'verification'.

- Discuss items/systems the function of which needs to be verified on a regular basis (e.g. car inspections) and describe the procedure.

- Take the CCP in Step 3 above and ask the trainees to set up a verification programme for it (key words are: hazards, criteria, monitoring devices).

Confidence with these definitions will encourage the trainees to use them in the following sessions when they come to the implementation of HACCP. Make sure that any other expression which might possibly cause uneasiness is also explained. Depending on the time available a workshop can be added to conduct a hazard analysis on a chosen product including critical parameters, suitable monitoring devices and verification procedures.

Implementing HACCP will often mean a 'cultural change' for a company. Understanding the language will certainly support the adaptation.

CHAPTER 8

How to Do It – Setting Up a HACCP System

This is possibly the most intense session of the whole course. Timing is therefore very important, and the trainer should check that the trainees' attention curve is at its peak.

As a warm-up for the subject the following exercises can be useful:

- Hold a brainstorming session to explain HACCP in one sentence.

Note for the trainer

Make a note of any key expressions. This exercise can also be modified. Suggest that a new colleague has never heard of HACCP and that, not being an academic person, he or she needs an easy 'matter-of-fact' explanation.

- Quote one of the 'classic' definitions of HACCP, e.g.

   HACCP is a systematic approach to the identification and assessment of the microbiological hazards and risks associated with food and the definition of means for their control. (ICMSF)

   Discuss this definition and compare it with a 'modern' definition of HACCP, e.g.

   HACCP is the simplest possible controls where they matter the most. (Mitchell, 1994)

Step 1: The seven principles of HACCP

The HACCP system consists of seven principles which outline how to set up, implement and maintain a HACCP plan. These seven principles have international acceptance and go back to publications of the NACMCF (1992) and the Codex Alimentarius Commission (1993). The trainees must understand and be able to explain the meaning of the HACCP principles by using the detailed knowledge they have gained in previous sessions.

The seven principles are as follows:

- Identify hazards and assess their severity and risk.

- Identify critical control points.

- Specify criteria to ensure control.

- Monitor critical control points.

- Establish corrective actions to be taken when monitoring indicates criteria are not met.

- Verify that the system is functioning as planned.

- Establish effective record-keeping procedures.

Note for the trainer

The meaning of each principle should be explained and understood thoroughly. The practical aspects of how a company sets up a HACCP system is discussed in the following step.

Step 2: How to do it

Setting up the team – 'the HACCP operators'

What makes a team? A team is characterised by

- joint intentions;

- joint efforts;

- joint skills.

The HACCP team has to represent:

- all production steps;

- all processes (including maintenance, cleaning and disinfection, etc.);

- all staff levels.

The differences between large companies and small enterprises will also be reflected in the team composition. However, the concept of the multifunctional team can also be applied in small companies where just one or two people are required for the job.

Exercise/discussion

You are considered a member of the HACCP team. What is your personal input? What can you contribute in terms of:

- technical knowledge;

- HACCP operating skills (e.g. monitoring, documenting, verifying, supervising).

Note for the trainer

Let the trainees discuss which skills are necessary to set up a HACCP system and therefore need to be represented in the team. Ask several trainees to describe themselves as part of the HACCP team. Discuss the possibilities of getting external advice if part of the know-how is not available within the company.

Describe your product – 'no product is the same'

Exercise/discussion

Chose a product from your company and give a full description, including all aspects relating to composition and distribution.

Note for the trainer

Ask for some volunteers to carry out the above task and let the remaining trainees put questions to them. Discuss the importance of having thorough product information including:

- source;

- ingredients;

- process;

- storage conditions;

- form of distribution.

Identify the intended use – 'use or abuse?'

This exercise is obviously closely related to the previous step and the two steps can easily be combined. It is, however, necessary to point out that the same product can be made differently according to different consumers' tastes.

Note for the trainer

The following is a useful example: consider a 'Pizza Margherita' as made by three different companies.

- In company A – the 'Ristorante Rosario' – the pizza is produced to order for the patrons of the restaurant where it is also consumed.

- In company B – 'Eddie's Pizza Delivery Service' – the pizza is produced following telephone orders and delivered to the client.

- In company C – 'Pizza Grande Ltd' – the pizza is produced as a pre-baked frozen convenience product to be purchased in retail markets and finally processed by the consumer.

Discuss how you can protect your product from unintended abuse by the consumer.

Construct a flow diagram – 'breaking up the process'

Trainees who are involved in quality management are usually familiar with the term 'flow diagram' and may be able to explain its meaning. It has to be emphasised that the word 'step' has a particular meaning in the context of HACCP as it refers not only to operations, processes or procedures but also to stages of the product, e.g. raw material, storage forms, etc.

Note for the trainer

Provide several examples of flow diagrams for different products, including at least one very simple, straightforward example and one rather complex one (such as that given in Appendix 1). Point out common steps (e.g. purchase, receipt of raw ingredients, storage, etc.).

Discuss the different situations to be found in:

- a large manufacturing company (straight product-specific flow charts modelled along the lines of a motorway – see, for example, Figure 8.1);

- a catering company (complex process-specific flow charts modelled along the lines of a railway station – see, for example, Figure 8.2).

Workshop

Construct a flow chart for a given product.

Note for the trainer

Choose a very easy and well known product such as a cup of tea (see Appendix 1) or a fried egg. Prescribe the ingredients but not the preparation. Divide the trainees into at least two different groups. Get the trainees to write the different steps on slips of paper and pin them to a board. Compare the results and discuss the differences.

Leave the charts to be continued/completed in a subsequent exercise.

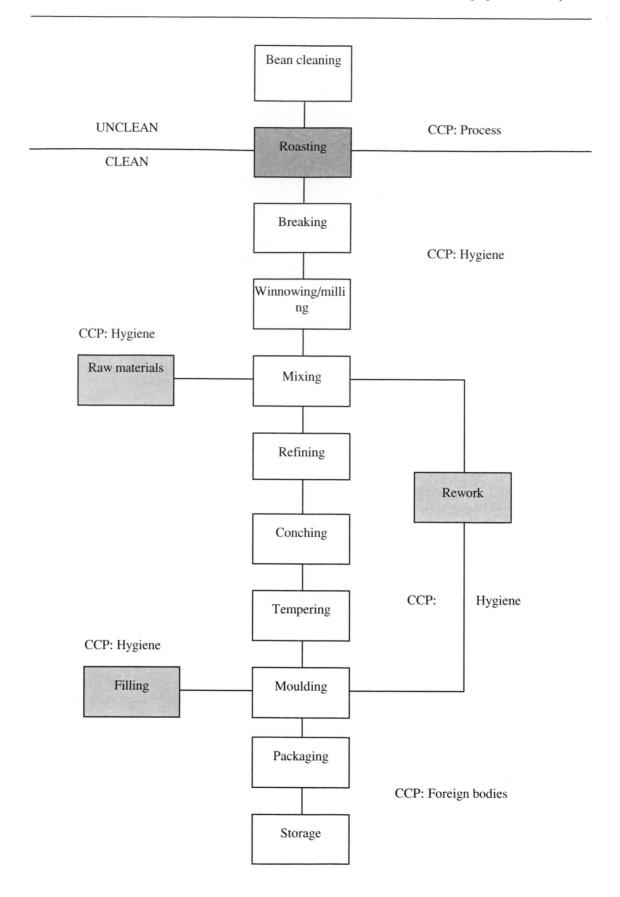

Figure 8.1 A product-specific flow diagram for the manufacture of chocolate.

(IOCCC: Hygiene Code for cocoa, chocolate and confectionery on the basis of HACCP)

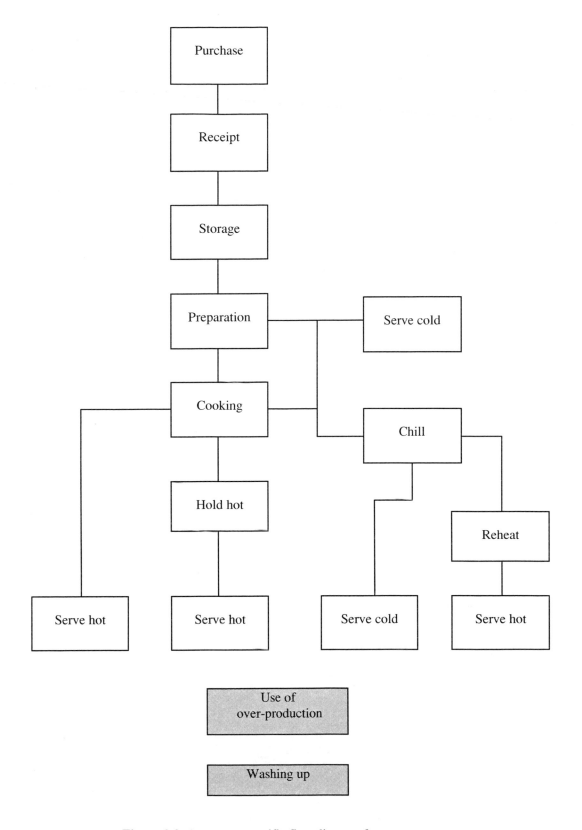

Figure 8.2 A process-specific flow diagram for a canteen.

Source: Adapted from the Department of Health, *Assured Safe Catering*, London.

On-site confirmation – 'first proof'

So far points the exercises can be regarded as the gathering of detailed information about product and process. It is, however, important that all this data is realistic and mirrors the 'real-life' situation on the shop floor.

Note for the trainer

Ask the trainees what they would do if they had a lot of paper information including flow charts on a product and wanted to review this data on the shop floor ('walking the line').

Identify hazards and preventative measures – 'confronting the risks'

With this point the course is now approaching the *first principle*. It may be worthwhile summing up the ground covered so far as this is going to be everybody's homework before they can start setting up their own HACCP plans!

Revision

Repeat the definition of 'hazard' and describe the different hazard categories. Put special emphasis on microbiological hazards.

Key words and concepts to emphasise are:

- microbiological, chemical and physical hazards;

- contamination;

- multiplication;

- survival of micro-organisms;

- preventative measures.

Workshop

Go back to the product flow charts on the pinboards and let each group conduct a hazard analysis listing:

- all hazards associated with each process step;

- all preventative measures available to control the hazards.

Compare and discuss the results. Make a list of preventative measures and categorise them into different group, e.g.

- measures against microbiological hazards (e.g. time and temperature controls);

- measures against chemical hazards (e.g. thorough product specifications, controlled storage of chemicals, etc.);

- measures against physical hazards (e.g. sieving, metal detectors, etc.);

- general controls (e.g. good hygiene practices).

Identify critical control points – 'climb the decision tree'

At this point the trainees are probably eager to discuss the CCPs. What they have learned so far is that it obviously takes a lot of preparatory work, i.e. gathering product details, drafting flow charts, identifying hazards and available preventative measures *before* they can start to think about the *second principle*.

Revision

Repeat the definition of 'critical control point'. Point out that:

- CCPs cover microbiological, chemical and/or physical hazards;

- steps dealing with quality issues, good-manufacturing practice or fraud will not be considered;

- each step in the process can be linked to one or more hazards;

- the control measures to be considered should be practicable and economically feasible.

For the purpose of the course it is recommended that you use the decision tree model to identify the CCPs, the main reason being that it forces the trainees to concentrate on both common sense and flexibility. Although you can use one of the classical decision tree models you may decide to use instead a modified approach (the 'decision ladder' – see Appendix 2).

Workshop

Go back to the product flow charts and the hazard analysis which you have already developed. Identify the CCPs of your process using the decision tree.

Note for the trainer

Select one trainee in each group to read out the questions of the decision tree starting with the first step (usually 'purchase of ingredients'). The CCPs are identified by applying the decision tree model to each hazard in turn until all hazards for a particular step have been dealt with. Then let them proceed to the next step.

You should point out that:

- different teams need not necessarily come up with the same CCPs;

- this is not a competition over which process has the most CCPs;

- a large number of CCPs may affect the economy and efficiency of the process.

Discuss the results (team presentation). If there have been any problems or difficulties demonstrate the decision tree for a given example, e.g. the microbiological hazards in meat preparation (see Appendix 2).

Note for the trainer

This first guided example (e.g. the 'cup of tea' or whatever simple example you have chosen) has now served its purpose and may be abandoned. However, depending on the amount of time available, you can continue using this example for the next three sections but it is recommended that you save the practical exercises for later (see Step 3 below).

Establish criteria and critical limits – 'what to control'

The course has now reached the *third principle* which provides an opportunity for the trainees to apply their knowledge and understanding of hazards, preventative measures and other criteria.

Revision

Define and discuss 'criteria', e.g. time, temperature, pH, a_w, concentration, particle size, microbiological counts in terms of their suitability and application. Bear in mind the following:

- Criteria are characteristics which must be specified to ensure the control of product safety.

- The defined criteria are meant to control the CCP. This can be achieved through:

  - the maintenance of certain parameters with a set value/target (e.g. chemical concentrations);

  - the maintenance of parameters with a target level which allows a certain tolerance or specified variation from the target level (e.g. temperatures);

  - operating practices which have to work reliably (e.g. visual controls).

Establishing criteria and setting up target levels and tolerances is probably one of the most difficult parts of the HACCP plan. The limits and tolerances have to be specified for each preventative measure in place and should adhere to the following principles:

- They should keep the CCP under control.

- They should be observable and measurable quickly and easily.

- If possible measurements should be taken on-line without interrupting the process.

- Measurements should be recorded in the simplest possible way.

Note for the trainer

Demonstrate some examples such as:

- cooking time/temperature combinations;

- pH of foodstuffs during preservation processes (i.e. pickling);

- particle size and conveyor belt speed for metal detectors;

- organoleptic parameters (e.g. visual appearance, texture).

Establish a monitoring system – 'looking after the CCPs'

The *fourth principle* is meant to demonstrate that a CCP is under control. Monitoring covers all kinds of observing, measuring and checking procedures.

Question and answer session

- What kind of monitoring procedures do you know?

- How do they work?

- What do you expect from your monitoring system?

Discuss the following definition:

> Monitoring is the measurement or observation at a CCP of the criteria which allows corrective actions to be taken. (MacDonald and Engel, 1996)

Monitoring also depends on responsibilities, i.e.

- *who* is to act;

- *when* the operator has to act;

- *how* the operator has to act.

Note for the trainer

Choose an easy example (i.e. a heating process) and go through the who, when and how with your trainees.

Establish corrective actions – 'saving your product'

The *fifth principle* may be well known to anybody involved in quality control but it may be completely alien to those with a 'let's hope and pray it never happens' attitude. It may be worthwhile remembering that in many day-to-day situations we have well established corrective actions, i.e.

- stomach rumbling indicates hunger → put in food;

- car tyre is flat → change to spare tyre and take to garage;

- water in bath tub is too hot → pour in cold water (or the other way round);

- alarm clock didn't work → phone office and pretend you're . . .

Of course some of these corrective actions may meet with approval whereas others are not suitable in every situation or shouldn't be applied in general.

Establishing corrective actions means that a specific action plan should be in place whenever a process comes to a point where the established criteria are not met. These actions will depend on the process and should, if possible, take place at a point where the product still can be 'restored', thus obviating the need for disposal.

Note for the trainer

Discuss different types of corrective actions. Let the trainees discover that there are different kinds of corrective actions:

- actions which 'save' the product (i.e. cook longer; increase temperatures, add preservatives);

- actions which rework or recycle the product (or change the intended use of the product);

- actions which dispose of the product.

Verify the system – 'reviewing strategies'

The *sixth principle* is something of a science in itself. Many systems need constant or regular verification to ensure that they are working properly. Verifying is therefore a 'maintenance tool' to keep a HACCP system in good working order.

Revision

Go over again what has been discussed about verification/reviewing procedures in the previous chapter.

- Which parts of the HACCP system need to be verified?

- Who should verify?

- When should they verify?

Verification covers two aspects:

- Are the HACCP procedures as originally applied still appropriate to the product/process hazards?

- Are the established monitoring procedures and corrective actions still being properly applied?

Verification can take place for two reasons:

- As part of a set regular pattern;

- following changes in the product, the process or the company.

Note for the trainer

Discuss potential changes, e.g. ingredients, equipment, processes, staff, newly emerging hazards.

Establish record keeping – 'written proofs/written confirmation'

The benefits of the *seventh principle* will be discussed in greater detail in Chapter 10on maintaining the HACCP system but it is still worthwhile discussing the reasons for keeping documentation. It needs to be pointed out that record keeping

- checks whether the system is successfully working;

- can show failure trends which may indicate that a certain CCP is out of control;

- helps the management to demonstrate that the HACCP principles have been properly applied;

- promotes customer confidence.

The following list provides the essential elements of record keeping and demonstrates how the HACCP principles are involved in the HACCP documentation:

- What is my *product* (specification, ingredients, formulation)?

- What is my *production* (flow chart)?

- Where are the *critical control points* and what are the *hazards* that need control? (*Principles 1 and 2*)

- What especially needs control? (*Principle 3*)

- How do I look after it? (*Principle 4*)

- What do I do if something goes wrong? (*Principle 5*)?

- When did I last check 'my' HACCP system as a whole, and did I find anything that needs changing/improving? (*Principle 6*)

- What have I changed and how did I modify 'my' HACCP according to the change? (*All principles*)

Step 3: Setting up a HACCP plan

It is now time to put the previous steps into practice and set up a HACCP plan. In the classroom situation it is only possible to carry out a condensed version, but it is still possible and will demonstrate that the trainees have successfully understood the course.

Workshop

Take a product of your choice and develop a HACCP plan explaining/listing:

- product description;

- product composition;

- intended use;

- flow chart/process steps;

- potential hazards;

- preventative measures;

- CCPs;

- criteria/critical limits to be observed at the CCPs;

- monitoring procedures at the CCPs;

- corrective actions;

- records in place (checklists; working orders, reports, etc.).

Note for the trainer

Select at least two different groups. The choice of product is up to your trainees, but make sure that at least one trainee is familiar with the chosen product and process. The HACCP plan is best demonstrated in table form (see Appendix 3) and such working sheets can be prepared in advance. For better demonstration purposes one sheet for each working group can be copied onto an overhead acetate. The flow chart should show the process broken into different steps which is again best performed and demonstrated using a pinboard. Identification of the CCPs should be carried out using a decision tree (see Appendix 2).

As this is going to be a lengthy workshop timing is an important factor so the examples which are chosen should not be too complicated. A recommended schedule taking approximately two hours (without a presentation) would be as follows:

- Product description – approx. 5 minutes.

- Product composition – approx. 5 minutes.

- Intended use – approx. 5 minutes.

- Flow chart/process steps – approx. 30 minutes.

- Potential hazards and preventative measures – approx. 30 minutes.

- CCPs including criteria/critical limits – approx. 30 minutes.

- Monitoring procedures, corrective actions and record keeping – approx. 15 minutes.

A shorter version lasting approximately one hour is possible if the trainees set up the flow chart and concentrate on one CCP only.

This workshop can be used as a conclusion to the session or it can be held over to the next session where it can be used to demonstrate HACCP plans for various food industries.

CHAPTER 9

HACCP for Different Food Industries

Knowing the seven principles of HACCP and having learnt how to set up a HACCP concept in 12 steps does not necessarily mean that the trainees are now able to transfer this knowledge immediately and without restriction to their own individual situations.

Learning 'how to HACCP' is like learning how to swim on your own: it is the practice that matters. No book will ever be able to teach somebody how to swim; equally a lot of theory will not make a HACCP expert. This is why every HACCP course must be based on exercises, workshops and demonstrations – in other words, needs to be as practical as possible.

Practical application of HACCP

Before applying HACCP principles in the daily working situation the theory needs to be adjusted to individual needs. This means now we need to look at the practical application of HACCP in different branches of the food industry.

There are two possible approaches as outlined below.

Method 1

The first approach is to look at the different types of industry which deal with different types of product, e.g.

- meat products (butchers, meat processors, etc.);

- dairy products;

- beverages (brewers, fruit juice manufacturers, etc.);

- bakery products (bakers, confectioners, etc.);

- fish;

- and so on.

A product-specific approach towards HACCP follows the 'classical' formulation of the HACCP concept, is relatively easy to comply with and has the advantage of focusing on typical hazards for special products.

The downside of it is obvious: this method will automatically concentrate on manufacturing processes and is therefore rather exclusive. Retail companies and caterers, for example, may be able to follow the approach but will not be able to identify completely with it.

Method 2

The second approach is to look at industries with different processes, e.g.

- manufacturers;

- retailers;

- caterers;

- transport companies.

This process-specific approach enables everybody to look at different companies *and* different product ranges. It is a form of 'HACCP made easy' as it facilitates the application of HACCP principles for both small and medium-sized companies in general and catering businesses in particular.

These approaches are looked at in more detail in the exercises which follow.

Step 1: A process-specific approach to HACCP

After they have concentrated on the production process for one particular product the trainees generalise what they have learned by looking at typical process steps and then adjusting their hazard analyses and risk assessments.

Question and answer exercise

Imagine a product going through the food chain *after* its primary production. There are several stages every product has to go through before it ends up on a consumer's table. Discuss the hazard potential of different process steps.

Key words to include her are:

- purchase;

- receipt of goods;

- storage;

- preparation;

- time/temperature-related processes;

- packaging;

- transport;

- display;

- serving.

Note for the trainer

Ensure the 'product' is as anonymous as possible. In order to conduct a proper hazard analysis you may wish to imply that this is going to be a high-risk product requiring specific temperature control. Point out typical time-related process steps (e.g. storage' transport). Relate physical, chemical and microbiological hazards to different stages of the product.

The exercise can be a guided question and answer session or – depending on the time available – a group exercise.

Step 2: The Assured Safe Catering model

Catering is probably the food business with the most diverse and complicated range of products. However, even here it is not only possible but relatively easy to apply the principles of HACCP if you take a process-specific approach as described by the guide booklet published by the Department of Health's *Assured Safe Catering* (1993). The booklet describes in detail a fairly straightforward system of hazard analysis for caterers.

The ASC model can be presented by the trainer in form of a lecture, as a flow chart demonstration or by using slides/training videos from the catering point of view. An introduction to Assured Safe Catering should be given even if no representative from the catering industry is present in the course as most companies are likely to have a staff canteen which must also operate following HACCP principles.

Step 3: Process-specific HACCP for different companies

Comparing different industries will enable you to:

- identify general process steps;

- point out individual industry-specific process stages.

Workshop

Carry out a process-specific HACCP on:

- a manufacturing company (i.e. baker, butcher, dairy producer);

- a retail company;

- a transport company;

- a caterer.

Identify typical CCPs, parameters and suitable monitoring techniques. The objective of the exercise is to point out:

- conformities;

- specialities.

Note for the trainer

The group dealing with the manufacturing process may alternatively go back the previous workshop (see p. 78) and look at it from a process-specific point of view.

Summary

Are there typical hazards/CCPs for the industries you have discussed? Are there general hazards/CCPs which will always need control (e.g. receipt of goods, temperature controlled storage, etc.)? As regards the different types of food businesses, do the trainees now feel able to spot potentially hazardous steps/stages in advance?

This session is another step in the 'HACCP familiarisation process'. It will, in the long term, also teach the trainees to become less dependent on the decision tree model.

CHAPTER 10

HACCP Maintenance – Keeping the Concept Alive

Many conventional HACCP courses will have finished by now. It is, however, essential not only to show your trainees how to set up a HACCP system but also to teach them how to 'work' it. A HACCP concept is like a living organism – it needs to be looked after if you want it to stay vital 24 hours a day.

Three important factors contribute to the support of and confirm the efficiency of a HACCP programme:

- documentation;

- verification (reviewing);

- auditing.

Step 1: Documentation

Documents are written evidence that preventative measurements are in place and working. The HACCP plan itself has to be regarded as the central document which is supported by daily, weekly or less frequent records. The difference between 'cardinal documents' (the HACCP plan, general instructions and written procedures, etc.) and 'assembly line' records needs to be understood as well as the relationship between documentation, monitoring and corrective actions.

Workshop

Pick one typical CCP (i.e. 'receipt of raw food') and give details of:

1.   its description/documentation in the HACCP plan;

2.   potential daily/online checks/records.

Discuss different forms of record keeping (e.g. checklists for visual checks; PC-controlled recording of physical or chemical parameters, data printouts, etc.).

Note for the trainer

Documentation must be adjusted to the needs and the size of the respective business. Small and medium-sized companies may do with a minimum of daily records as long as their HACCP plan contains all the necessary information. Depending on your delegates you can discuss the proposition in the following exercise.

Workshop

Set up a documentation scheme for a small company which requires a *minimum* of daily record keeping. Which of the already existing documents (e.g. delivery notes) can be adapted as HACCP documents?

Step 2: Verification

The purpose of verification is to ensure that the HACCP system is continuously functioning as planned. HACCP is a 'living system' – it deals with technology, people, food and live hazards, all of which can change and will change sooner or later.

Verification needs to be seen as a multiple confirmation process:

- to confirm effective implementation of the HACCP plan;

- to confirm the accuracy of processes and/or parameters;

- to confirm the reliable and proper functioning of monitoring procedures.

Verification can be carried out by both internal and external experts/verifiers. Verification of the HACCP plan can be achieved as a whole or broken into several activities, e.g. looking at particular CCPs, reviewing deviations and corrective actions, random sampling and testing of product stages, etc. Some reasons for verification activities can be predicted and scheduled in advance; others will be a reaction to unforeseen changes.

Key terms and concepts to include in your discussions are:

- HACCP plan;

- preventative measures;

- reviewing;

- validation;

- critical limits;

- risk factors;

- record keeping.

Question and answer session

What are the typical elements in verification? The discussion should include mention of the following terms and activities:

- verification schedule;

- review of the HACCP plan;

- verification of flow diagrams;

- review of CCP records;

- visual inspections;

- review of documentation;

- review of critical limits;

- on-site review.

Discuss the following quotations:

> Verification is the use of supplementary information and tests to ensure that the HACCP system is functioning as planned. (Bryan, 1992)

> Verification is investigative auditing. (Pierson and Hudak-Roos, 1995)

Workshop

Set up a verification schedule listing:

- reasons

- activities

- frequencies

- responsibilities

for reviewing.

Step 3: Auditing

Auditing is a verification process. It can be defined as a systematic and independent examination to determine whether existing activities and related results comply with the original plan thus showing whether the original plan has been implemented effectively. This can be stated more simply:

> Are you doing what you say you do – and is it appropriate?

Every company may be faced with different types of audit:

- internal audit (company verifies its own systems);

- external audit (company verifies external systems, e.g. those of a supplier);

- extrinsic audit (company is audited by customer);

- independent audit (company is audited by a third body, e.g. a certification institution).

Auditing means visiting or being visited – looking or being looked at. This may sound simple, but these visits need to be structured and thoroughly planned. An audit involves observation, questioning, listening and – occasionally — sample testing.

Workshop

A   You are visiting a potential new supplier who claims to have a HACCP system in place. What do you want to see/check/verify on your first visit?

B   An important potential client is coming to visit your company. What are you prepared to show them?

Note for the trainer

This exercise can be carried out as two workshop groups confronting each other: group A is auditing group B. Any discrepancies in the audit schedules can be discussed in a role play.

On-site auditing involves more than just looking at the HACCP plan itself because the auditor will automatically get an impression of the whole scenario. This puts a new focus on the programmes that are required to support the HACCP plan, e.g. the cleaning schedules, personal hygiene, pest management, etc.

Discussion

What evidence can a visual inspection reveal?

This discussion leads us to the essential importance of hygiene principles and their significance for the HACCP plan.

CHAPTER 11

HACCP and the Concept of Hygiene

It has become clear now that HACCP like many other management systems depends on people:

- people who set it up;

- people who manage it;

- people who control it;

- people who review it.

If it wasn't for these people we would not need HACCP training courses! One of the HACCP keywords which is never mentioned among the classic HACCP definitions is *commitment*. Commitment is based on four factors:

- conviction;

- motivation;

- responsibility;

- prerequisites.

To establish conviction and motivation is the task of the trainer; supporting it depends on the attitude of the company. To establish responsibilities is part of the HACCP team recruitment process. This leaves the prerequisites: what needs to be in place to build up an efficient HACCP system.

Question and answer session

You have been appointed as new hygiene manager of your company, and your first job is to set up a HACCP system. What do you need to be in place (or to introduce) before you can start?

Key terms and concepts to cover include:

- cleaning schedules;

- personal hygiene rules;

- staff training;

- pest management;

- waste management;

- technological prerequisites;

- maintenance procedures for machinery and equipment;

- prevention of cross-contamination;

- foreign body and glass control.

The models described in the steps below stress the interactions between basic hygiene prerequisites and HACCP.

Step 1: The hygiene jigsaw

A hygiene programme can be considered as a jigsaw, with several elements linking into each other to form a whole image (see Figure 11.1). The pieces of the jigsaw are the different components of a food business:

- premises, equipment and utensils;

- people;

- processes;

- products.

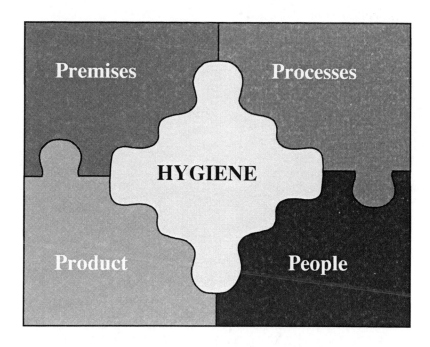

Figure 11.1 The hygiene jigsaw.

Obviously each element has an influence on each of the others. The size and layout of the premises and the technology employed determine the actions and the amount of space for movement of the people who work there. The people themselves have an effect on the equipment through their work and maintenance activities. Both premises and people determine the kind of processes used inside the company, whether they be for the production itself or the cleaning procedures, pest control, upkeep of the building, etc. The interaction between these three factors then determines the quality and safety of the product.

Step 2: The hygiene house

The next step is to integrate these elements into the HACCP concept. The ideal model to use here is the 'hygiene house' (after Untermann, 1998 – see Figure 11.2). Setting up a food safety system follows the same steps as building a house: laying the foundations, erecting the walls and, finally, building the roof. This matches the different levels in a food business:

- Level 1 (ground level – the static level): conditions of premises and equipment.

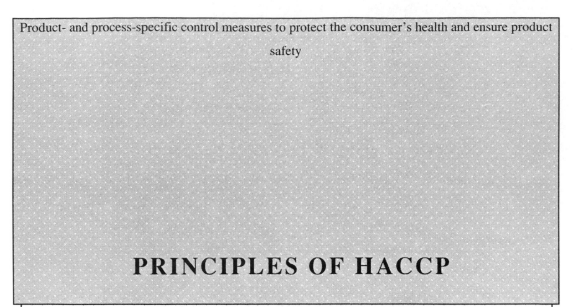

Product- and process-specific control measures to protect the consumer's health and ensure product safety

PRINCIPLES OF HACCP

FUNDAMENTAL HYGIENE REQUIREMENTS

- • Cleaning and disinfection

- • Pest control

- • Temperature and humidity controls on production and storage areas

- • Separation of clean and unclean processes to prevent cross contamination

- • Personal hygiene

PREMISES HYGIENE

Equipment, utensils, technological prerequisites

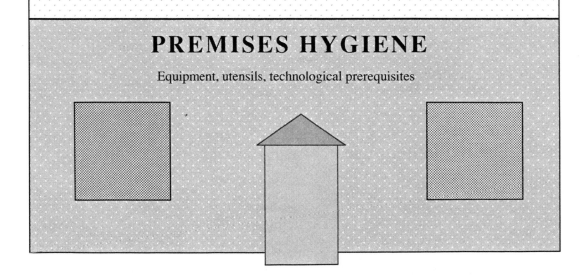

Figure 11.2 The hygiene house.

(Adapted from Untermann, 1998.)

- Level 2 (the 'house' – the dynamic level): basic hygiene prerequisites, e.g. preventative measures against cross-contamination, personnel hygiene, cleaning and disinfection, pest control).

- Level 3 (the 'roof' – the safety level): product- and process-specific preventative measures based on hazard analysis.

This 'hygiene house' can be built by any kind of business regardless of product range or size. The model also describes how to proceed: like building a proper house you need to start with the foundations – nobody builds a house by starting with the roof. HACCP concepts that have been left without the proper foundations are left 'hanging in the air'!

The Untermann (1998) model can be extended by setting a chimney representing quality management. Remember that a chimney on a rooftop is not like a swirl of cream on a piece of cake but is a system of its own that needs to be supported by all three levels below.

Step 3: The hygiene play

The last model, summarised in Figure 11.3, compares the introduction of a HACCP system to the preparation for and performance of a theatre play.

- Setting the stage – establishing the premise of hygiene.

- Setting the properties – taking care of adequate design and maintenance of equipment and utensils, and introducing controls and preventative measures.

- Training the actors – establishing food hygiene training for staff.

- Rehearsing the play – HACCP team training.

- The play itself – *The Principles of HACCP* (hopefully on for a long season!).

This model – 'HACCP – The Drama' points out clearly the importance of the people who have to work the system. Hi-tech modern equipment will not help to save your system if your actors have forgotten their cues and lines.

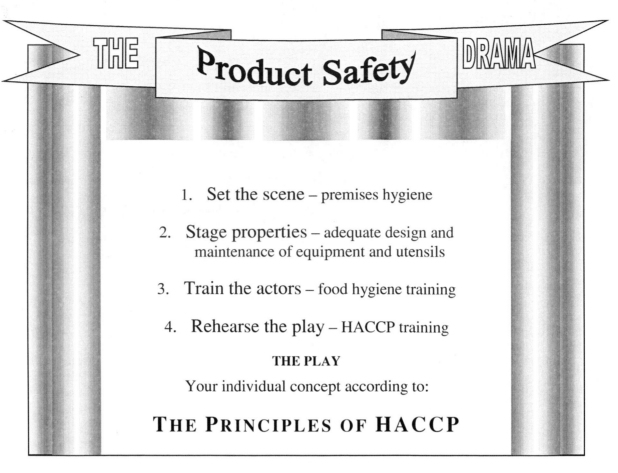

(Prompters: Codex Alimentarius, NACMCF, Food Hygiene Directive 93/43)

Figure 11.3 The hygiene play.

Step 4: HACCP and the quality concept

Many companies have a quality management system in place before they even begin thinking about HACCP. In this case it is important to point out the differences between the two systems, find out what they actually have in common and discuss ways to link both systems together.

Question and answer session

What is food quality? Key concepts to discuss include:

- taste;

- freshness;

- price;

- nutrition;

- pollution;

- image;

- 'value for money'.

Quality relates to the standards set by consumers' expectations whereas HACCP has regard for safety standards. HACCP principles, as required by the Food Safety Regulations 1995, are *obligatory*; quality management is a – voluntary – tool of competition. The situation is summarised in Figure 11.4.

HACCP is top of the quality pyramid!

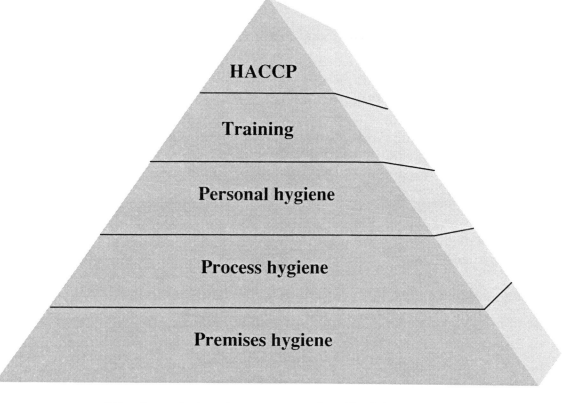

The foundation layers must be GMP/GHP

Figure 11.4 The hygiene pyramid.

(Adapted from an idea by A. Halligan, 1998)

Question and answer session

What do HACCP and quality management have in common? Key terms and concepts to include are:

- target parameters;

- monitoring;

- corrective actions;

- documentation;

- reviewing procedures;

- preventative actions;

- control points.

Note for the trainer

Companies with a well established quality apparatus should be encouraged to check existing documents for their usability in the HACCP system. However, it should be pointed out that:

- HACCP means the assurance of product safety;

- quality management, on the other hand, means the assurance of a constant level of quality.

- HACCP can be operated without quality management;

- modern quality management, on the other hand, cannot be operated without HACCP.

CHAPTER 12

Special HACCP Courses

Ever since the implementation of HACCP principles became compulsory for the food industry other sectors providing services to the food industry have become aware of the benefit of having HACCP systems and of being able to consult food businesses when building up their systems. Other industry branches making auxiliary goods for the food industry such as manufacturers of primary and secondary packaging materials have found that their customers expect them to adjust their own quality systems according to the principles of HACCP. Representatives of these groups can easily attend a standard HACCP seminar – which may indeed benefit from their presence and special points of view – but it is also worthwhile setting up special training courses for these target delegates.

However, there are a number of key points to bear in mind:

- The classic HACCP concept is meant for *food* safety only.

- Manufacturers of food-related products and auxiliary items as well as service providers may find their purposes sufficiently served by a thorough hazard analysis conducted on their products/processes/services.

- Any critical control point identified needs to be related to *food* safety.

- Hygiene prerequisites are fundamental essentials and need to be in place before starting the hazard analysis.

- Risk assessment on any potential hazard can and should be carried out.

- The supplier/customer relationship is an important factor to ensure than one HACCP system links smoothly into the other.

In the following we look at three different target groups:

- pest control operators;

- food packaging manufacturers;

- food control officials.

HACCP for pest control operators

Modern pest control means integrated pest management (IPM) which involves:

- close cooperation with the customer;

- preventative measures;

- permanent monitoring

- re-examination and measurement to prevent reinfestation after control actions.

Apart from a basic knowledge of HACCP principles (see Chapters 6, 7 and 8) the modern pest controller needs to find and identify his part in the hygiene system of his customer. It is important to draw a distinct line between HACCP principles and IPM principles, although this may be difficult as 'HACCP jargon' has already entered into pest control terminology. For example:

- Hazard analysis:

  – the PCO needs to understand that pests represent microbiological hazards as well as physical contaminants;

  – the PCO needs to accept that pest control substances are potential chemical hazards.

- Control points:

  – 'pest control points' are not necessarily identical with CCPs as they can represent monitoring devices, bait stations, insect-o-cutors, etc.;

  – pest control parameters may depend on pest biology, monitoring techniques or working method of chemicals.

- Monitoring and documentation:

- the aim of pest prevention is pest-free conditions. Monitoring and documentation need to describe the situation of the company in terms of potential pest infestation;

- corrective actions are obviously pest control strategies to fight an unwanted infestation.

- Verification: pest control systems need to be reviewed on a regular base to make sure that:

    - the existing control measures are still effective;

    - the pest control apparatus can deal with potential new infestations;

    - the company staff is following the PCO's instructions.

Pest control should be part of the hygiene prerequisite programme as the HACCP system needs to rely on the fact that sufficient pest control measurement is in place!

HACCP for food packaging manufacturers

There is a close relationship between the packaging of food and potential risks like the migration of unwanted substances from the packaging material into the product. These risks have drawn the food manufacturer's attention towards this 'forgotten ingredient'.

Food packaging manufacturers are in a slightly different situation from the PCO as the former are dealing with products which are intended to come into direct contact with food and thus need to fulfil certain requirements. Some of these requirements may be quality issues dictated by the customer while others are safety parameters. A hazard analysis can easily be carried out on the basis of what adverse effects packaging materials and packaging ingredients may have on the food product.

The hygiene jigsaw (see Chapter 11) supports the idea of introducing a solid hygiene management system before concentrating on product- and process-specific criteria. The following approach is recommended:

- The inert nature of most packaging materials as well as of many primary processes such as extrusion, thermoforming, injection moulding, etc. gives a rather safe starting point although typical hazards still need to be identified and assessed.

- Most hazards in food packaging production stem from the production environment (including people!).

- A reliable hygiene network (including hygiene of premises, cleaning schedules, maintenance techniques, personal hygiene, pest control, etc.) will keep these hazards under control.

- The seven principles of HACCP can be applied provided that the aim is to protect the end consumer.

- A HACCP-type approach should focus on product- and process-specific hazards.

- Most hazards are likely to take the form of physical contaminants.

- Staff training in elementary food hygiene is vital.

HACCP for food control officials

Checking the efficiency of HACCP systems is increasingly becoming a duty of food safety enforcers. Obviously such persons need to be equipped with both elementary and detailed knowledge of HACCP, but what else do they need to know?

Food control officials should have detailed knowledge of:

- health risk analysis:

    - hazard identification;

    - hazard characterisation;

    - exposure characterisation;

    - risk characterisation;

- risk estimation:

    - categorising food businesses according to their risk potential;

- conducting assessments and critical examinations of existing control measures;

- identifying alternative control options.

They also need to be familiar with the principle of risk-based inspections. This will involve:

- identification of potential hazards;

- risk assessment;

- control system assessment;

- scoring systems.

However, they should *never* develop systems for the company!

As a final comment, it is worthwhile considering afresh the three major aims of any food business (MacDonald, 1997):

- to make a profit;

- to make safe food;

- to stay within the law.

The point of intersection is the application of the HACCP principles.

APPENDIX 1

HACCP Workshops

A simple HACCP workshop

This is a simple example designed to allow trainees to become confident in working with the HACCP system by applying it to a simple food processing operation with which everyone is familiar – making a cup of tea. (Note that since the author's first application of this simple group exercise at least 25 different versions of 'making a cup of tea' have been developed!)

Workshop

1.   Construct a flow diagram for making a cup of tea using *all* the ingredients listed and select from the equipment as necessary.

2.   List *all* the hazards associated with each step of the process.

3.   List any preventative measures to control these hazards.

4.   Identify the CCPs using the decision tree model (or decision ladder as appropriate – see Appendix 2).

5.   Which criteria would you wish to monitor?

Ingredients

- Tea bag

- Whole pasteurised milk

- Sugar

- Water

Equipment

- Kettle

- Cup

- Spoon

- Tea pot

(*Source*: MacDonald, 1990)

A complex HACCP workshop

This example deals with the preparation of a chicken salad as a menu item in a restaurant. The accompanying flow diagram shows nicely how three different product lines come together. Depending on the time available for the workshop, the students can either develop a flow diagram of their own of start with the one provided in Figure A1.1.

Workshop

1. Please list *all* hazards (microbiological, chemical and physical) but then concentrate on microbiological hazards. If you require to make assumptions please do so but note what they are and why you have made them.

2. Construct a flow diagram for the process (or use Figure A1.1).

3. List *all* the hazards associated with each step of the process.

4. List any preventative measures to control *microbiological* hazards.

5. Identify the CCPs using the decision tree (or decision ladder as appropriate – see Appendix 2).

6.   Which criteria would you wish to monitor?

7.   List all targets and tolerances and who should be responsible for them.

8.   Suggest which documentation should be kept.

Product description

One quarter of roast chicken (250–300 g) accompanied by 3 lettuce leaves, 6 cucumber slices (2 mm thick), 2 sliced tomatoes, 1 sliced egg,1 small sliced onion, sliced red and green peppers, lemon slice, sprinkled with 5 g cress and accompanied by 15 g home-made mayonnaise.

Intended use

To be served in a restaurant.

Ingredients

- Chicken quarters (from uncooked frozen whole chicken)

- Lettuce

- Cucumbers

- Tomatoes

- Water cress

- Boiled eggs

- Small onion – sliced

- Red and green peppers – sliced

- Lemon slice

- Home-made mayonnaise – fresh eggs, lemon juice, vegetable oil, spices

(*Source*: Engel and MacDonald, 1997)

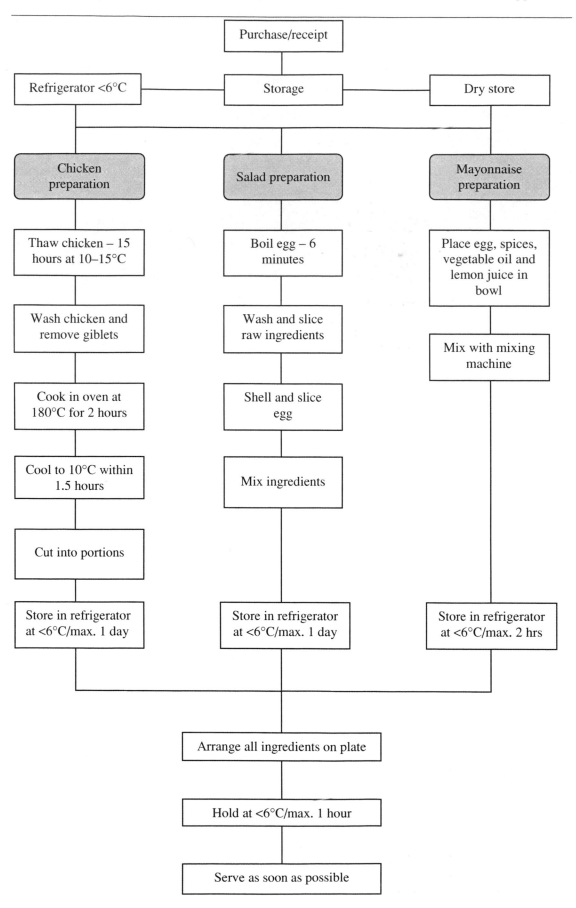

Figure A1.1 Flow diagram for the preparation of chicken salad.

APPENDIX 2

The Decision Tree Model

The classic decision tree

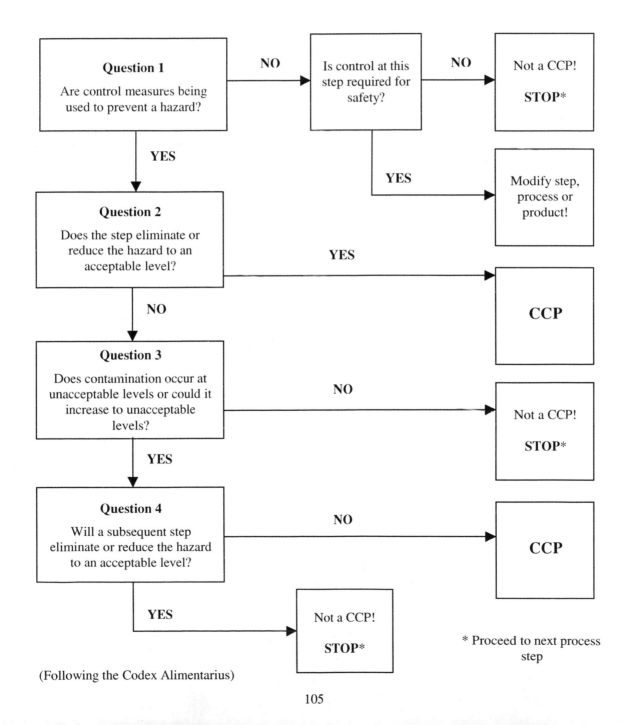

(Following the Codex Alimentarius)

105

The decision ladder – a simplified decision tree

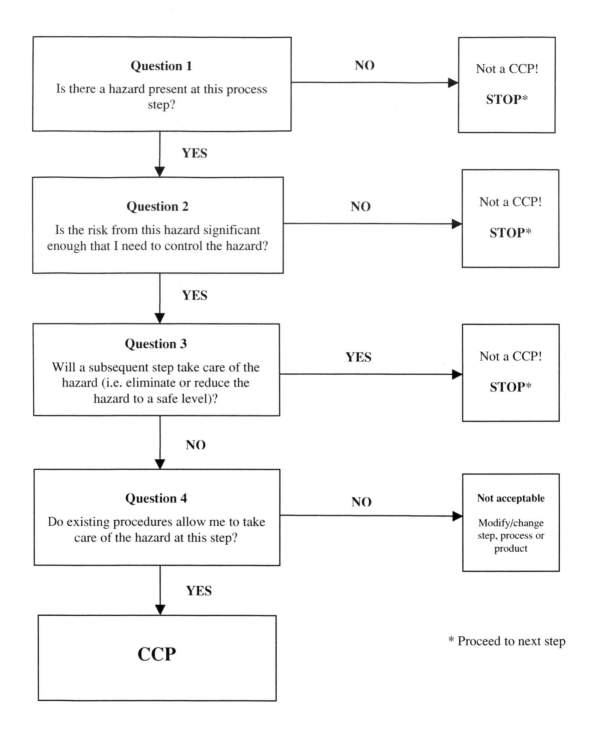

(*Source*: Engel and MacDonald, 1998)

HACCP Working Sheet

Process step	Hazard	Preventative measures	CCP?	Critical limit	Monitoring	Corrective measures	Documentation

Source: Engel and MacDonald (1997).

REFERENCES

Bryan, F. (1992) *Hazard Analysis Critical Control Point Evaluations. A Guide to Identifying Hazards and Assessing Risks Associated with Food Preparation and Storage*. Geneva: WHO.

Campden Food & Drink Research Association (UK) (1992) *HACCP: A Practical Guide*, Technical Manual No. 38. CFDRA.

Chartered Institute of Environmental Health (1977) *Hazard Analysis Principles and Practice Certificate/Training Support Material*. London: CIEH in association with Premier Health Consultants Ltd.

Codex Alimentarius Commission (1993) *Guidelines for the Application of the HACCP System*. Alinorm 93/13A.

Codex Alimentarius Commission (1995) *General Principles for Food Hygiene*. Alinorm 95/13, Annex.

Codex Alimentarius Commission (1996) *Report of the 29th Session of the Codex Committee on Food Hygiene*. Alinorm 97/13A, Appendix II.

Department of Health (1993) *Assured Safe Catering. A Management System for Hazard Analysis*. London: HMSO.

de Winter, R. F. J. (1998) 'The Role of Interactive Workshops in HACCP Training in a Multinational Environment, *Food Control*, vol. 9, nos 2–3.

Dillon, M. and Griffith, C. (1997) *How to Audit. Verifying Food Control Systems*. M.D. Associates.

Engel, D. (1997) *Lean HACCP – Hazard Analysis Demystified*, in Proceedings of the Meat Hygiene Conference of the International Food Hygiene and International Poultry Production, Stoneleigh.

Engel, D. (1998) 'Teaching HACCP – Theory and Practice from the Trainer's Point of View', *Food Control*, vol. 9, nos 2–3.

MacDonald, D. and Engel, D. (1996) *A Guide to HACCP – Hazard Analysis for Small Businesses*. Doncaster: Highfield Publications.

Mayes, T. (1994) 'HACCP Training', *Food Control*, vol. 5, no. 3.

Mitchell, R. T. (1995) 'How to HACCP', *British Food Journal*, vol. 94, no. 1, pp. 16–20.

Mortimore, S. and Wallace, C. (1994) *HACCP – A Practical Approach*. London: Chapman & Hall.

National Advisory Committee for Microbiological Criteria in Foods (NACMCF) (1992) 'Hazard Analysis and Critical Control Point System', *International Journal of Food Microbiology*, vol. 16, pp. 1–23.

Pierson, M. D. and Hudak-Roos, M. (1995) *Hazard Analysis and Critical Control Point (HACCP) Verification Manual*. TFiS.

Royal Environmental Health Institute of Scotland (1996) *Principles of HACCP Certificate* (Syllabus). REHIS.

Untermann, F. (1998) 'Microbial Hazards in Food', *Food Control*, vol. 9, nos 2–3.

World Health Organisation (1993) *Report of the WHO Consultation on Hazard Analysis Critical Control Point Training*, WHO/FOS/93.2. Geneva: WHO

World Health Organisation (1993) *Training Consideration for the Application of the Hazard Analysis Critical Control Point System to Food Processing and Manufacturing*, WHO/FNU/93.3. Geneva: WHO.

World Health Organisation (1996) *Training Aspects of the Hazard Analysis Critical Control Point System (HACCP)*, WHO/FNU/FUS/96.3. Geneva: WHO.